The Red Lantern Festival
A Play Based on a Chinese Folktale

Janet Stutley
Illustrated by Xiangyi Mo and Jingwen Wang

Contents

What Are Folktales? 3

Cast of Characters 4

Scene 1 Yuan's Family Home 6

Scene 2 The Palace Kitchen 8

Scene 3 The Palace Throne Room 14

Scene 4 The Palace Kitchen 18

Scene 5 The Palace Balcony 20

Scene 6 Yuan's Family Home 26

Scene 7 The Palace Kitchen 28

The Facts Behind the Story 30

Read, Research, and Write 31

Extend Your Reading 32

What Are Folktales?

Folktales are stories that are told over and over again. We do not know who first created them, but they have become well-known over many years. Folktales come from many different parts of the world, and sometimes they give us information about a culture.

The play in this book is based on an old folktale from China. It tells us how a special Chinese festival began.

3

Cast of Characters

Yuan, a young girl

Shen
Yuan's father

Fen
Yuan's mother

Lok
Yuan's brother

Shuo, an advisor to
the Emperor Wu Di

Emperor Wu Di

Narrator

- **Palace People**
- **People of the City**

Scene 1

Yuan's Family Home

Narrator: In China, on the first full moon of the year, there is a great festival. This is the story of how that tradition began.

A long, long time ago in ancient China, there lived a young girl named Yuan.

She loved her family, but she had to leave them and go away to work as a cook at Emperor Wu Di's palace. Sadly, she said goodbye.

Yuan: I am sorry to have to leave you, my family.

Fen: We are sorry that you have to go. But it is an honor to have a job at the palace!

Shen: We will miss your good cooking.

Lok: Yes, especially your wonderful rice dumplings!

Yuan: *(hugging Lok)* I have heard that the Emperor is very fond of rice dumplings, too, little Lok.

Fen: When will you come and see us again?

Yuan: The Emperor does not allow anyone to leave the palace. But I will try to find a way.

Scene 2

The Palace Kitchen

Narrator: Six months passed. Yuan worked hard at the palace, and people were kind to her. She even became friends with Shuo, an advisor to the Emperor.

One day, Yuan was working in the kitchen when Shuo came in.

Yuan: Hello, Shuo. *(She bows.)*

Shuo: Hello, Yuan. *(He bows.)* You are looking sad today.

Yuan: I miss my family. I like my job cooking for the Emperor. But I wish I could see my family sometimes.

Shuo: Yes, it is hard being away from them. I will try to think of some way to help you.

Yuan: That would be wonderful! If I could just visit them for one day, it would make me so happy.

Shuo: Leave it to me. I'll see what I can do.

Narrator: It did not take long for Shuo to think of a plan. The next day, he told Yuan about his idea.

Yuan: Good morning, Shuo. *(She bows.)*

Shuo: Good morning, Yuan. *(He bows.)* I have thought of a plan to help you.

Yuan: Really? Please tell me!

Shuo: The Emperor is very proud of his great city. And he knows that the best way to keep it safe is to please the gods.

Yuan: So what is your plan?

Shuo: I will advise the Emperor that the God of Fire is very angry and wants to burn down the city.

Yuan: The Emperor will want to know how to prevent this.

Shuo: I will tell him that we should have a celebration in honor of the God of Fire. There could be a parade with beautiful red lanterns. It will look like a blazing fire and the God of Fire will be happy.

Yuan: And we could have many fireworks, too!

Shuo: Yes! And while the Emperor is busy with the celebration, you will be able to leave the palace. You can spend the night with your family. He won't even notice that you are gone.

Yuan: When will we have this celebration?

Shuo: I will tell the Emperor that we must have the celebration on the first full moon of the year.

Yuan: That is in ten days! Can everything be ready by then?

Shuo: I will begin making plans with the Emperor this afternoon.

Yuan: I can hardly wait to hear what happens!

Scene 3

The Palace Throne Room

Narrator: And so, that very afternoon, Shuo went to see the great Emperor Wu Di.

Emperor Wu Di: Come in, Advisor Shuo. You have something to tell me?

Shuo: *(bowing deeply)* Yes, Emperor. You know I study the stars. The stars tell me that the God of Fire is very angry and wants to destroy the city.

Wu Di: This is terrible news! What can we do to prevent this?

Shuo: I have an idea. We must put on a great celebration in honor of the God of Fire. We must have a parade of red lanterns through the streets of the city. They will glow like fire.

Wu Di: Then we could have a fireworks display!

Shuo: Our celebration will make the God of Fire happy and the city will be saved.

Emperor Wu Di: When should we do this?

Shuo: On the night of the first full moon of the year, Emperor. Everyone in the city and the palace should take part. The greater the celebration, the better! Let's also prepare a feast with special foods. I will ask the cooks to make delicious rice dumplings.

Emperor Wu Di: We must begin getting ready at once! *(He stands and claps his hands to get everyone's attention.)* We are going to have a big celebration in ten days, on the night of the full moon. There will be a lantern parade and fireworks. Everyone must be involved.

Palace People: *(bowing deeply)* Certainly, Emperor Wu Di!

Emperor Wu Di: Tell the cooks they will be making many rice dumplings!

Palace People: *(bowing deeply)* At once, Emperor Wu Di!

Shuo: *(smiling)* I am sure that the God of Fire will be very pleased.

Scene 4

The Palace Kitchen

Narrator: And so, the people of the palace and the city began to make beautiful red lanterns. They gathered the rice for the dumplings. Amazing fireworks were planned. Yuan and Shuo met once again.

Yuan: Your plan is working! Everyone is so busy that I could almost slip away now!

Shuo: Wait until the night of the celebration. Make your special dumplings and take some to the Emperor. Once he is feasting, you can go.

Yuan: Yes, of course. I am terribly excited!

Shuo: Perhaps you can make some extra dumplings to take home to your family. No one will notice if a few are missing.

Yuan: Shuo, you think of everything! Thank you.

Scene 5

The Palace Balcony

Narrator: The night of the full moon finally arrived. Everything was ready for the big celebration.

The Emperor and Advisor Shuo stood on the palace balcony, looking over the city. Many people were already walking in the streets. They were carrying beautiful red lanterns. Yuan arrived carrying a plate of dumplings.

Shuo: Emperor, all is happening as we planned. Let us begin the feast with these delicious rice dumplings.

Yuan: *(kneeling in front of the Emperor)* For you, Emperor. I hope you will enjoy them.

Wu Di: I'm sure I will. Now it is time for
the lantern parade! Advisor Shuo,
wave the red banner so the townspeople
know to begin.

Shuo: Yes, Emperor. *(He waves a banner.)*

Narrator: And so, the lantern parade began. Everyone carried their lanterns through the streets. It looked like there were hundreds of fires blazing.

Shuo: Look at all the lanterns. They look like a river of fire flowing around the town!

Wu Di: It is a beautiful sight indeed.
And these dumplings are delicious!

Narrator: Shuo nodded to Yuan,
who was standing back in the shadows.
Yuan left the palace and hurried out of
the city and toward her home.

Narrator: Then the fireworks display began. Beautiful colored sparks filled the night sky. All the people cheered.

Wu Di: Advisor Shuo, do you think the God of Fire will be happy?

Shuo: Yes, sir. I can tell by the stars that he is very happy to be honored in this way. And are you enjoying the celebrations, Emperor?

Wu Di: I have enjoyed them so much that I am going to make a new law. *(He turns to speak to the people.)* Every year, on the night of the first full moon, we will hold the celebrations again!

People of the City: Hurray! Hurray! Hurray!

Wu Di: And we will call it the Festival of the Red Lanterns!

People of the City: Hurray! Hurray! Hurray!

Scene 6

Yuan's Family Home

Narrator: Meanwhile, Yuan was at home with her family. She had brought a big basket of rice dumplings for all of them to eat.

Yuan: Dear mother, father, little brother. I am so pleased to see you!

Fen: And we are so happy to see you!

Shen: How did you get away?

Yuan: My friend, Shuo, helped me. He is a palace advisor. It was his clever plan to have this great celebration. I could get away because the Emperor is busy watching the parade.

Lok: I love fireworks and lanterns. Everyone must be so happy!

Yuan: Yes, little Lok. Everyone is happy. And now, let us eat these dumplings that I have brought for you.

Scene 7

The Palace Kitchen

Narrator: Yuan spent many hours with her
family. Then she said goodbye. She hurried
back to the palace in time to make the
Emperor's breakfast. Her friend, Shuo, was
waiting for her in the palace kitchen.

Shuo: Did you hear the good news? The Emperor has announced that the Lantern Festival will be held every year at this time.

Yuan: So I will be able to visit my family every year!

Shuo: Yes!

Yuan: Thank you, Shuo! I am lucky to have you as my friend.

Narrator: And so it is, that on the first full moon of every year, the Chinese people still celebrate the Red Lantern Festival. They light red lanterns, set off fireworks, and eat rice dumplings. The dumplings are a special reminder of the girl who wanted so much to visit her family.

The History of Fireworks

Fireworks were invented in China over 1,000 years ago. The Chinese discovered how to make an explosive powder, called gunpowder. To make fireworks, they put gunpowder into tubes made from stems of bamboo plants. The gunpowder was lit using a burning fuse, and the fireworks exploded in the air with loud noises and bright sparks.

Fireworks are still a special part of many festivals all over the world.

Write a Paragraph About Festivals

Think about the Red Lantern Festival and another festival or celebration, such as Independence Day.

- Draw a Venn diagram, like the one below. Put the name of a festival in each circle.
- Write special things about each festival in the correct circle.
- How are the festivals the same? Write your ideas where the circles overlap.
- Use your diagram to help you write a paragraph about the two festivals. Tell how they are the same and how they are different.

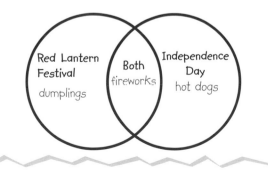

Think About the Story

In *The Red Lantern Festival,* Yuan works at the Emperor's palace.

- What does Yuan like about her life at the palace? What doesn't she like?
- Who is Yuan's friend at the palace? How does he help her?
- What does the Emperor decide on the night of the festival?

To learn more about ancient civilizations, read the books below.

SUGGESTED READING
Windows on Literacy
The Great Pyramid
The Aztecs

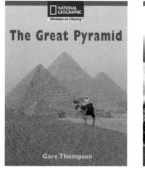

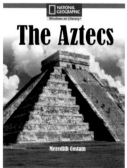